D0597052

A Quick Word with

BETH
MOORE

A Quick Word with

BETH
MOORE

Scriptures & Quotations from
BELIEVING GOD

By faith we understand that the universe was created by the word of God, so that what is seen has been made from things that are not visible.

Hebrews 11:3

Faith is the way
believers jump on
board with God and
participate in countless
wonderful things He
has a mind to do.

I will give you rain
at the right time, and the
land will yield its produce,
and the trees of the field ·
will bear their fruit.

Leviticus 26:4

God has far more in
mind than bringing forth
one kind of fruit from
your life. The harvest
God desires to produce
has the potential for
abounding variety.

God is able to make
every grace overflow
to you, so that in every
way, always having
everything you need,
you may excel in
every good work.

2 Corinthians 9:8

I am freed to know
that my God is huge,
and my God is able. So
I know if I don't get
what I asked from Him,
if I'll cooperate, I'll get
something bigger.
I'll know that a greater
"yes" is in progress.

For we are His
creation—created in
Christ Jesus for good
works, which God
prepared ahead of
time so that we
should walk
in them.

Ephesians 2:10

If you can't imagine
God ever delivering you
from the corruption of
evil desires and bringing
forth a great harvest
through your life, you've
bought into the lie that
God's promises don't
apply to you.

How much more will
the blood of the Messiah,
who through the eternal
Spirit offered Himself
without blemish to God,
cleanse our consciences
from dead works to serve
the living God?

Hebrews 9:14

I know I'm going to make it to heaven because I've trusted Christ as Savior, but I want to make it to my Canaan on the way. I want to finish my race in the Promised Land, not in the wilderness.

In every situation
take the shield of faith,
and with it you will be
able to extinguish the
flaming arrows of
the evil one.

Ephesians 6:16

When we respond
to attacks of doubt,
distortion, and deceit
with the truth of God's
Word, the fiery dart is
extinguished and
the enemy takes
another hit.

I pray that the eyes
of your heart may be
enlightened so you may
know what is the hope
of His calling . . . and
what is the immeasurable
greatness of His power
to us who believe.

Ephesians 1:18—19

God exerts an
incomparable power in
the lives of those who
continue believing in
Him. Nothing on earth
compares to the strength
God is willing to interject
into lives caught in the
act of believing.

I was not a
prophet or the son
of a prophet . . . but the
Lord took me from
following the flock
and said to me, "Go,
prophesy to My
people Israel."

Amos 7:14–15

Sometimes God demands radical measures when He wants to bring about radical results. I may look silly, but I'm a walking miracle experiencing the power of God.

You have commanded
that Your precepts be
diligently kept. If only my
ways were committed to
keeping Your statutes!

Psalm 119:4–5

If God said it,
I want to believe it.
If God gives it, I want to
receive it. If God shows it,
I want to perceive it.
If Satan stole it, I want
to retrieve it.

These are written
so that you may believe
Jesus is the Messiah,
the Son of God,
and by believing you
may have life in
His name.

John 20:31

Surrounded by a society
that spouts many gods
but at best nobly agrees
to equate them, you and
I can know that the Lord
is God. We're not going
anywhere of profound
eternal significance
until we know.

Blessed be the God
and Father of our Lord
Jesus Christ, who has
blessed us with every
spiritual blessing in the
heavens, in Christ.

Ephesians 1:3

Blessing is not defined by
ease, worldly possessions,
or stock market successes.
Blessing is bowing down
to receive the expressions
of divine favor that in
the inner recesses of the
human heart and mind
make life worth
the bother.

They have hands,
but cannot feel; feet, but
cannot walk. They cannot
make a sound with their
throats. Those who make
them are just like them,
as are all who trust
in them.

Psalm 115:7–8

I don't think the biggest
threat to our theology is
humanism or the host
of world religions. Our
biggest threat is cut-and-
paste Christianity. If man
places his faith in a god he
has recreated in his own
image, has he placed his
faith in God at all?

Most certainly, the
mystery of godliness is
great: He was manifested
in the flesh, justified in
the Spirit, seen by angels,
preached among the
Gentiles, believed on
in the world, taken
up in glory.

1 Timothy 3:16

We cannot tame the Lion of Judah. There is a mystery, a wonder, and, yes, even a wildness about God we cannot take from Him. If we can come up with a God we can fully explain, we have come up with a different God from the Bible's.

I tell you that you
are wrong in this matter,
since God is greater than
man. Why do you take
Him to court for not
answering anything
a person asks?

Job 33:12—13

God doesn't sit
on His throne saying,
"Oops, I wouldn't have
done that, but now that
you have, I guess I'll go
with it." Remember, God
doesn't work for us.
We work for God.

Return to a stronghold,
you prisoners who have
hope; today I declare
that I will restore
double to you.

Zechariah 9:12

God's specialty is raising
dead things to life and
making impossible things
possible. You don't have
a need that exceeds His
power. Faith is God's
favorite invitation to
R.S.V.P. with proof.

I will give you the keys of the kingdom of heaven, and whatever you bind on earth is already bound in heaven, and whatever you loose on earth is already loosed in heaven.

Matthew 16:19

God would empower His children to bind untold evils and strongholds if we'd believe Him and cooperate with Him. Where does this begin? With biblical answers to the pivotal question, "Who do you say that I am?"

Lord, I have heard the report about You; Lord, I stand in awe of Your deeds. Revive Your work in these years; make it known in these years.

Habakkuk 3:2

As Savior, He saves. As Deliverer, He delivers. As Redeemer, He redeems. As Master, He assumes authority. As Bread of Life, He provides. As Almighty, He exerts divine strength.

With the pure You prove Yourself pure, but with the crooked You prove Yourself shrewd.

2 Samuel 22:27

God seems to like saying,
"Oh, yes I will" to the
"Oh, no He won'ts."
He doesn't mind at all
proving His own people
wrong to prove His
Word right.

I give this land to your offspring, from the brook of Egypt to the Euphrates River: the land of the Kenites, Kenizzites, Kadmonites, Hittites, Perizzites, Rephaim, Amorites, Canaanites, Girgashites, and Jebusites.

Genesis 15:18–21

From the moment God issued the promise of land to Abram, He described its occupants as quickly as its perimeters. Our Promised Lands are characterized by the presence of victory, not the absence of opposition.

Now to Him who is able
to do above and beyond
all that we ask or think—
according to the power
that works in you—
to Him be glory in the
church and in Christ
Jesus to all generations,
forever and ever.
Amen.

Ephesians 3:20–21

I want a thousand things
for my children, and I ask
without hesitation. But
I want nothing more than
for God to be glorified.
The only thing that will
matter forever is the
glory that came to God
through their lives.

The world is unable to
receive Him because it
doesn't see Him or know
Him. But you do know
Him, because He remains
with you and will
be in you.

John 14:17

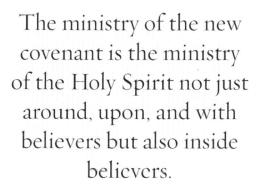

The ministry of the new covenant is the ministry of the Holy Spirit not just around, upon, and with believers but also inside believers.

For I consider that
the sufferings of this
present time are not
worth comparing with
the glory that is going
to be revealed to us.

Romans 8:18

Suffering is a
compulsory part of
human existence in a
terribly fallen world. The
difference for believers is
that our suffering need
never be in vain.

He said to me, "I will make you fruitful and numerous; I will make many nations come from you, and I will give this land as an eternal possession to your descendants to come."

Genesis 48:4

The enemy is standing on your God-given ground daring you to take possession of it. Are you going to let him have it? Or are you going to claim your inheritance? Possession is the law of the Promised Land. Red Rover, go over.

As for me, I will never boast about anything except the cross of our Lord Jesus Christ, through whom the world has been crucified to me, and I to the world.

Galatians 6:14

If you want to be full of faith, don't argue with a legalist! Love them. Serve side by side with them, if God wills. But don't judge them, and don't argue with them. Unbelief is highly contagious.

He was crucified in
weakness, but He lives
by God's power. For we
also are weak in Him,
yet toward you we will
live with Him by
God's power.

2 Corinthians 13:4

Has God placed you in a
position that seems to stir
up every insecurity you
have? Take it personally.
He's stirring it up to
scoop it out, often one
spoonful at a time.

Someone will say,
"You have faith, and
I have works." Show me
your faith without works,
and I will show you faith
from my works.

James 2:18

Those who presently and actively believe God are prompted to make wiser and healthier decisions. Authentic faith cannot help but act. How we behave overwhelmingly flows from what we deeply believe.

The fear of
the Lord is pure,
enduring forever;
the ordinances of
the Lord are reliable
and altogether
righteous.

Psalm 19:9

Most of us believe
God is who He says He is,
but we are less quick to
believe He can do what
He says He can do.
Ironically, however,
God can do what He
says He can do precisely
because He is who
He says He is.

How happy those
whose lawless acts are
forgiven and whose sins
are covered! How happy
the man whom the Lord
will never charge
with sin!

Romans 4:7–8

I suppose all of us
who have histories of
heinous sin cling to any
affirmation that God
really can forgive and
use those who have
terrible pasts.

We know that no one
is justified by the works
of the law but by faith in
Jesus Christ. And we have
believed in Christ Jesus,
so that we might be
justified by faith in Christ
and not by the works
of the law.

Galatians 2:16

Our faith is in a God
of grace who forgives the
authentically repentant
and then "no, never"
counts their sins against
them anymore. All that
time I thought God was
counting my sins, and He
was counting my faith as
righteousness instead.

He gave Himself
for us to redeem us
from all lawlessness and
to cleanse for Himself a
special people, eager
to do good works.

God can relentlessly
credit our faith as
righteousness without
concern that we'll take
advantage of the freedom.
He knows faith that does
not lead to obedience is
all talk and no walk.

On that day it will be said, "Look, this is our God; we have waited for Him, and He has saved us. This is the Lord; we have waited for Him. Let us rejoice and be glad in His salvation."

Isaiah 25:9

I am utterly
convinced that any "no"
an earnestly seeking child
of God receives from the
Throne is for the sake of
a greater "yes," whether
realized on earth
or in heaven.

The Word became flesh
and took up residence
among us. We observed
His glory, the glory as the
One and Only Son from
the Father, full of grace
and truth.

John 1:14

When Christ came
to earth, He stepped
His feet into the "one
and only" shoes and, for
the first time in history,
they were a perfect fit.
Wriggle your bare toes
and celebrate that He's
been wearing them
ever since.

All the more, those parts of the body that seem to be weaker are necessary. And those parts of the body that we think to be less honorable, we clothe these with greater honor.

1 Corinthians 12:22–23

Christ left us too much
to do to leave it up to a
chosen few. You are an
honored part of His body,
and your contributions
add up. God's math
specializes in addition
and multiplication, not
subtraction and division.

Now may the God of peace Himself sanctify you completely. And may your spirit, soul, and body be kept sound and blameless for the coming of our Lord Jesus Christ.

1 Thessalonians 5:23

To pick up the
Sword of the Spirit
without the Shield of
Faith is to shrivel and
dry up in the desert of
legalism. To pick up the
Shield of Faith without
the Sword of the Spirit is
to try walking by faith
on quicksand.

The Lord is certain
to bless you in the land
the Lord your God is
giving you to possess as
an inheritance—if only
you obey the Lord
your God.

Deuteronomy 15:4–5

Sometimes we have to
exercise faith to believe
that obedience to God in
a difficult situation will
ultimately bear fruit, even
though it looks as though
it might immediately
cause hardship.

You son of the Devil,
full of all deceit and
all fraud, enemy of all
righteousness! Won't
you ever stop perverting
the straight paths
of the Lord?

Acts 13:10

Don't think for a moment
Satan is going to slow
down when he sees you in
the way. He has an arsenal
of psychological weapons
to keep your feet off
promised ground.

We personally had
a death sentence
within ourselves so
that we would not trust
in ourselves, but in
God who raises
the dead.

2 Corinthians 1:9

Our insistence that
"I could never survive
if that happened to me"
is not only an insult to
people who have already
survived something
similar. It's an insult
to a wonderful thing
called grace.

When the disciples
saw Him walking on the
sea, they were terrified.
"It's a ghost!" they said,
and cried out in fear.
Immediately Jesus spoke
to them. "Have courage!
It is I. Don't be afraid."

Matthew 14:26—27

Faith is never the
denial of reality. It is
belief in a greater reality.
The reason you don't
have to buckle to fear
and discouragement is
the presence of God in
the middle of your
circumstances.

Because he is
lovingly devoted to
Me, I will deliver him;
I will exalt him because
he knows My name.

Psalm 91:14

Satan has no right to exercise authority over us, but he hopes we're too ignorant regarding Scripture to know it. Knowing and claiming God's Word when attacked blows the head off enemy forces.

If you remain in Me
and My words remain
in you, ask whatever you
want and it will be done
for you. My Father is
glorified by this: that
you produce much
fruit and prove to
be My disciples.

John 15:7–8

Whether or not you want to admit it aloud, God has gifted you out of His glorious grace and for His name's sake. Christ has spoken over your life as His present-day disciple.

Just then, a woman
who had suffered from
bleeding for 12 years
approached from behind
and touched the tassel on
His robe, for she said to
herself, "If I can just
touch His robe, I'll
be made well!"

Matthew 9:20–21

Do you feel like you've
failed God in some way?
Are you too scared or too
discouraged to try again?
Then hear these words:
God will not fail you.
Grab onto the hem of His
garment, and find the
healing and grace to go
where He leads.

The word of God is living
and effective and sharper
than any two-edged
sword, penetrating as far
as to divide soul, spirit,
joints, and marrow; it is a
judge of the ideas and
thoughts of the heart.

Hebrews 4:12

Don't miss the crucial tie between the Word of God and the people of God in this verse. God not only told us that His Word is alive, effective, and powerful on its own, He insisted that it is alive, effective, and powerful in us.

It is plain that you are
Christ's letter, produced
by us, not written with
ink but with the Spirit
of the living God; not
on stone tablets but
on tablets that are
hearts of flesh.

2 Corinthians 3:3

Nothing is a greater
threat to the enemy
than a believer with the
Word of God living
and active upon her
tongue, readily applied
to any situation.

My word that comes
from My mouth will
not return to Me empty,
but it will accomplish
what I please, and will
prosper in what I
send it to do.

Isaiah 55:11

God doesn't speak just
to hear the sound of His
own voice. Interestingly,
neither does He speak
to be heard by others.
He speaks in order
to accomplish.

Let the message about
the Messiah dwell richly
among you, teaching
and admonishing one
another in all wisdom,
and singing psalms,
hymns, and spiritual
songs, with gratitude
in your hearts
to God.

Colossians 3:16

Believe God to
accomplish and achieve
something eternal and
intentional through your
Scripture meditation
every single day. How
about something moving
into your life with some
positive baggage
for a change?

Now may the God of
peace . . . equip you with
all that is good to do His
will, working in us what
is pleasing in His sight,
through Jesus Christ, to
whom be glory forever
and ever. Amen.

Hebrews 13:20–21

When all is said
and done, the biggest
sacrifices of our lives
will be when we chose
our own way and
forfeited God's
pleasing will
for us.

Be diligent to present
yourself approved to God,
a worker who doesn't
need to be ashamed,
correctly teaching the
word of truth. But avoid
irreverent, empty speech,
for this will produce an
even greater measure
of godlessness.

2 Timothy 2:15–16

Frivolous arguments
can dilute spiritual truths
into human logic. To the
degree that we debate
matters of faith, we could
find ourselves drained of
it. We are not called to
debate faith but to do it,
to be nouns turned into
verbs. Presently.
Actively.

Consider ships: though
very large and driven by
fierce winds, they are
guided by a very small
rudder wherever the will
of the pilot directs. So
too, though the tongue is
a small part of the body,
it boasts great things.

James 3:4–5

James compares
the tongue to a small
rudder with the power
to steer a large ship.
Our words are potent no
matter how we use them,
but what would happen
if we allowed God to
take hold of them?

Now this is the confidence we have before Him: whenever we ask anything according to His will, He hears us. And if we know that He hears whatever we ask, we know that we have what we have asked Him for.

1 John 5:14–15

Something dramatic happened when I sensed one day that, frankly, God was bored with my prayer life. He seemed to say, "My child, you believe Me for so little. Don't be so safe in the things you pray. Who are you trying to keep from looking foolish? Me or you?"

I assure you: If you have faith the size of a mustard seed, you will tell this mountain, "Move from here to there," and it will move. Nothing will be impossible for you.

Matthew 17:20

If a mountain moves,
God moved it. He simply
invited us to join Him by
allowing us to exhale a
powerful breath of the
Spirit. Having the faith to
tell a mountain to move
and asking God to move
the mountain are not
opposing concepts.

I protested, "Oh no, Lord
God! Look, I don't know
how to speak since I am
only a youth." Then the
Lord said to me: "Do not
say: I am only a youth, for
you will go to everyone
I send you to and speak
whatever I tell you."

Jeremiah 1:6–7

Stop looking at others as being more spiritual than you and just start believing God! He's not looking for spiritual giants. God is looking for believers who believe for a change.

The Lord takes
pleasure in His people;
He adorns the humble
with salvation. Let
the godly celebrate in
triumphal glory; let
them shout for joy
on their beds.

Psalm 149:4–5

Would you be offended if
I told you that I not only
think God is awesome,
wonderful, and faithful,
but I also think He is fun?
Those who take the faith
out of spiritual living
have taken the fun
out of life.

Who among you fears
the Lord, listening to the
voice of His servant?
Who among you walks
in darkness, and has no
light? Let him trust in the
name of the Lord; let him
lean on his God.

Isaiah 50:10

People can play it
safe if they want, but
I like living out on a limb
with God. I've put all my
hopes and my faith in
Him. I have absolutely
nothing else to
hang on to.

As it is written:
"Look! I am putting a
stone in Zion to stumble
over, and a rock to trip
over, yet the one who
believes on Him
will not be put
to shame."

If you pray that God will move a mountain and He doesn't, or you have the faith to tell a mountain to move and it won't, assume Christ wants you to climb it instead and see Him transfigured. Either way, the mountain is under your feet.

I am able
to do all things
through Him who
strengthens me.

Philippians 4:13

We can do
all things through
Christ who strengthens
us, but frankly we
won't if we're
too afraid
to try.

Each of the four living
creatures had six wings;
they were covered with
eyes around and inside.
Day and night they never
stop, saying: "Holy, holy,
holy, Lord God, the
Almighty, who was,
who is, and who
is coming."

Revelation 4:8

Today you and I
stand before the same
throne the prophet
Isaiah approached in his
glorious vision. God is
just as holy. Just as high
and lifted up. The train
of His robe still fills
the temple, and the
seraphs still cry,
"Holy!"

In his hand was a glowing coal that he had taken from the altar with tongs. He touched my mouth with it and said: "Now that this has touched your lips, your wickedness is removed, and your sin is atoned for."

Isaiah 6:6–7

We need not hang our heads and beg. All we need to do is lift up our faces and ask. May Jesus touch our lips again with coals from the altar and set our tongues aflame with His holy fire.

Remember these
things, Jacob, and Israel,
for you are My servant;
I formed you, you are My
servant; Israel, you will
never be forgotten by Me.
I have swept away your
transgressions like a
cloud, and your sins
like a mist.

Isaiah 44:21–22

God never forgets
His promises to us.
In turn, He intends for
His children never to
forget His faithfulness to
fulfill them. A powerful
motivation for believing
God in our present is
remembering how He's
worked in our past.

You reveal the path
of life to me; in Your
presence is abundant joy;
in Your right hand are
eternal pleasures.

Psalm 16:11

No sin, no matter how
momentarily pleasurable,
comforting, or habitual, is
worth missing what God
has for us.

Take words of
repentance with you
and return to the Lord.
Say to Him: "Forgive all
our sin and accept what
is good, so that we may
repay You with praise
from our lips."

Hosea 14:2

Every believer needs
second chances. Some of
us need lots of them. God
looks upon our hearts and
knows whether we have
any authentic desire to
be different or if
we're all talk.

The Lord your God
is testing you to know
whether you love the
Lord your God with
all your heart and
all your soul.

Deuteronomy 13:3

Everyone who has been
delivered from bondage
will also experience times
of testing. I believe God
continues to test us in
an area until we pass.
Sometimes He even
seems to insist
on an A.

I no longer live,
but Christ lives in me.
The life I now live in the
flesh, I live by faith in
the Son of God, who
loved me and gave
Himself for me.

Galatians 2:20

As long as we wear these
cumbersome suits of
flesh, we are not going to
be supermen flying high
in the sky of faith. We are
called to something far
more elementary:
to walk by faith.

I call heaven and earth
as witnesses against you
today that I have set
before you life and death,
blessing and curse.
Choose life so that you
and your descendants
may live.

Deuteronomy 30:19

We know we're coming
full circle with God when
we stand at a very similar
crossroad where we made
such a mess of life before,
but this time we take a
different road.

Dear friends, when
the fiery ordeal arises
among you to test you,
don't be surprised by it,
as if something unusual
were happening to you.

1 Peter 4:12

I don't know a single
person who truly seems to
bear the mark of God's
presence and power in his
or her life who hasn't
been asked by God to be
obedient in a way that
was dramatically painful.

You took off your
former way of life, the
old man that is corrupted
by deceitful desires; you
are being renewed in the
spirit of your minds.

Ephesians 4:22–23

Though we were totally changed on the inside when we were made new creatures in Christ, our minds often take time to be renewed. We're far more likely to *act* like the old man of sin when we still *feel* like the old man of sin.

Clean out the
old yeast so that you
may be a new batch,
since you are unleavened.
For Christ our Passover
has been sacrificed.

1 Corinthians 5:7

If you are still
wearing any kind of
reproach from your past,
God wants to remind you
of the cross of Christ,
your Passover Lamb,
and memorialize the
victory it bought you.

Position yourselves, stand still, and see the salvation of the Lord. He is with you, Judah and Jerusalem. Do not be afraid or discouraged. Tomorrow, go out to face them, for the Lord is with you.

2 Chronicles 20:17

Fighting the good fight
of faith takes energy!
So do self-pity, anger,
unforgiveness, and
self-loathing. Each of
us must decide where
we're going to put our
energy when the battle
grows fierce.

The commander
of the Lord's army said
to Joshua, "Remove the
sandals from your feet, for
the place where you are
standing is holy."
And Joshua did so.

Joshua 5:15

If I could get a clue about the greatness of God, I'd be mortified by all the times He told me to do something, and the record showed, "And Beth did not do so." Help me, Lord.

When God fixed
the weight of the wind
and limited the water by
measure . . . He said to
mankind, "Look! The
fear of the Lord—that is
wisdom, and to turn from
evil is understanding."

Job 28:25, 28

God wants us to seek
Him and find Him. He
wants to draw us close
and find security in Him.
But He also wants us to
appreciate the greatness
and majesty of who He is
and the gift of the cross to
grant us bold access.

You must be like
people waiting for their
master to return from the
wedding banquet so that
when he comes and
knocks, they can open the
door for him at once.

Luke 12:36

You can still believe God
for something dramatic
and miraculous. But
what's a believer to
do in between these
dramatic revelations?
The day-in, day-out
fundamentals,
that's what.

I cry aloud to the Lord;
I plead aloud to the Lord
for mercy. I pour out my
complaint before Him;
I reveal my trouble to
Him. Although my spirit
is weak within me, You
know my way.

Psalm 142:1—3

I don't know about you,
but I tend to be a lot
gutsier in my vocalized
prayers, because hearing
them with my own ears
often ignites my heart
and mind all the more.

The person who
has entered His rest
has rested from his own
works, just as God did
from His. Let us then
make every effort to enter
that rest, so that no one
will fall into the same
pattern of disobedience.

Hebrews 4:10–11

Though God could
have thought the entire
cosmos into existence
in a millisecond, instead
He brought it about
with great patience in
six distinct increments.
Then rested. Then later
insisted that His children
do the same.

Hold on to the pattern of sound teaching that you have heard from me, in the faith and love that are in Christ Jesus. Guard, through the Holy Spirit who lives in us, that good thing entrusted to you.

2 Timothy 1:13–14

Sometimes I feel like the phrases I habitually use in prayer are surely getting old to God. In reality, as long as He sees a genuine heart, He never gets tired of some of the same old words and practices that flow from it.

Because of the Lord's
faithful love we do not
perish, for His mercies
never end. They are new
every morning; great is
Your faithfulness! I say:
The Lord is my portion,
therefore I will put my
hope in Him.

Lamentations 3:22–24

God's mercies have
existed through all of
eternity, yet Scripture
tells us they are new every
morning. A new day with
all its fresh challenges
gives an old practice
of faith new life.

All mankind has
seen it; people have
looked at it from a
distance. Look, God
is exalted beyond our
knowledge; the number
of His years cannot
be counted.

Job 36:25–26

I don't care
how intelligent the
deceiver seems or how
well-meaning and sincere
his or her doctrine. If in
our pursuit of greater
knowledge, God seems to
have gotten smaller, we
have been deceived.

After the seventh
time, the priests blew
the trumpets, and Joshua
said to the people, "Shout!
For the Lord has given
you the city."

Joshua 6:16

I never know when my present Jericho is going to fall. I just know that I'm to keep believing and keep marching. When the time is complete, the wall is going to collapse.

Set your minds on
what is above, not on
what is on the earth. For
you have died, and your
life is hidden with the
Messiah in God. When
the Messiah, who is your
life, is revealed, then you
also will be revealed
with Him in glory.

Colossians 3:2–4

Some of the most adventurous endeavors you'll have with God may be too difficult at the time to enjoy, and by the time the party comes, you may smell too bad to go. Ah, but after a shower and a good look back . . .

Let us not tempt Christ
as some of them did, and
were destroyed by snakes.
Nor should we complain
as some of them did,
and were killed by
the destroyer.

We can expend so much energy whining about the unfairness of our situation that we have nothing left to invest in the real fight.

Then you will delight
yourself in the Lord,
and I will make you ride
over the heights of the
land, and let you enjoy
the heritage of your
father Jacob.

Isaiah 58:14

I assure you,
God and I have made
some memories together.
Hard ones. Good ones.
Astounding ones.
You don't have to know
God long to make
memories with Him.

See to it that no
one falls short of the
grace of God and that no
root of bitterness springs
up, causing trouble and
by it, defiling many.

Hebrews 12:15

If Satan can turn us on
God, turn us on others,
or turn us on ourselves,
we won't turn on him. If
we keep fighting within
ourselves and losing our
own inner battles, we'll
never have the strength
to stand up and fight
our true enemy.

Moses said, "Please,
let me see Your glory."
He said, "I will cause
all My goodness to pass
in front of you, and I
will proclaim the name
Yahweh before you."

Exodus 33:18–19

Moses' encounter
with God in this scene is
unmatched in Scripture.
Why did Moses get to
experience such a thing?
Maybe because he had
guts enough to ask.

Indeed, we have
all received grace after
grace from His fullness,
for although the law was
given through Moses,
grace and truth came
through Jesus Christ.

John 1:16–17

This you can take to the spiritual bank: life is not fair. And there is someone to blame: Jesus Christ. And wouldn't I be stupid to miss that?

I will make them and
the area around My hill a
blessing: I will send down
showers in their season—
showers of blessing. The
trees of the field will give
their fruit, and the land
will yield its produce; My
flock will be secure
in their land.

Ezekiel 34:26–27

Sometimes God requires
us to follow a fair amount
of repetition for a
considerable amount of
time until He deems a
season complete. Then all
of a sudden, He seems to
do something profound
or miraculous, and we
can't figure out what
changed.

Clap your hands,
all you peoples; shout to
God with a jubilant cry.
For the Lord Most High
is awe-inspiring, a great
King over all the earth.

Psalm 47:1–2

You can experience the unmatched exhilaration of partnering with God in divine triumph. Yes, the stakes are high. The cost is high. But I'll promise you this: there is no high like the Most High.

Be imitators of God,
as dearly loved children.
And walk in love, as the
Messiah also loved us and
gave Himself for us, a
sacrificial and fragrant
offering to God.

Ephesians 5:1—2

The One who
adopted us into His
royal family has called
us to live according to
our legacy. We are to
literally live love.

Therefore,
let everyone who is
faithful pray to You at
a time that You may
be found. When great
floodwaters come, they
will not reach him.

Psalm 32:6

Sometimes
I jump up and down.
Sometimes I go prostrate
to the ground. Sometimes
I pray Scripture. Other
times I pray moans and
groans. But pray, I must.
It's God's will even
when I can't tell if it's
changing a thing.

The idolaters eagerly
seek all these things, and
your heavenly Father
knows that you need
them. But seek first the
kingdom of God and His
righteousness, and all
these things will be
provided for you.

Matthew 6:32–33

A big difference exists
between trying to
manipulate God to give
us what we want, and
cooperating with God
so He can give us
what He wants.

Keep in mind Jesus Christ, risen from the dead, descended from David, according to my gospel. For this I suffer, to the point of being bound like a criminal; but God's message is not bound.

2 Timothy 2:8—9

God sends His Word
forth, and it never returns
void, unchaining the soul
of every person with the
courage to believe it.
May we commission one
another to spend our
lives devouring it.

Since we have the
same spirit of faith in
accordance with what is
written, "I believed,
therefore I spoke,"
we also believe, and
therefore speak.

2 Corinthians 4:13

Believing God is what closes the gap between our theology and our reality. Maybe what we believe doesn't so much make us *what* we are as *how* we are.

When you do good and
suffer, if you endure, it
brings favor with God.
For you were called to
this, because Christ also
suffered for you, leaving
you an example, so that
you should follow
in His steps.

1 Peter 2:20–21

All that will matter
about our earthly lives
when we receive our
heavenly inheritance is
whether we fulfilled our
callings and allowed God
to fulfill His promises.

Afterwards, Samuel
took a stone and set it
upright between Mizpah
and Shen. He named it
Ebenezer, explaining,
"The Lord has helped
us to this point."

1 Samuel 7:12

I am a woman
with a human nature
heavily given to sin, but
I have not lived out of
that powerful old nature
in a long time. We are
making it, God and I,
one day at a time.

We always pray for
you that our God will
consider you worthy of
His calling, and will, by
His power, fulfill every
desire for goodness
and the work of faith.

2 Thessalonians 1:11

Faith is not something
you have. It's something
you do. This kind of faith
can turn a noun into an
action verb quicker
than you can say,
"See Spot run."

How great is
Your goodness that
You have stored up for
those who fear You,
and accomplished in
the sight of everyone
for those who take
refuge in You.

Psalm 31:19

God is looking
for stewards who are
willing to bind their own
unbelief in the mighty
name of Jesus and loose
a fresh anointing of faith
onto the topsoil of earth.
Are you game?

Therefore since we
also have such a large
cloud of witnesses
surrounding us, let us
lay aside every weight
and the sin that so easily
ensnares us, and run
with endurance the
race that lies
before us.

Hebrews 12:1

May your line stay
straight and steady.
May your eyes remain
fixed on Jesus, the Author
and Finisher of your faith,
who awaits you at the
finish line. And may the
path between your today
and your eternity be
strewn with stones of
remembrance.